ImagineIF Libraries
Kalispell, Montana

PREVIEW

There were bodies everywhere. Skeletons, to be exact. They were scattered all over Hardin, Missouri.

The Crisis

The Missouri River had overflowed its banks. The waters swept through Hardin, destroying homes and buildings— and digging up the dead.

The Horror
The local cemetery was in ruins. The flood had unearthed nearly 600 coffins. Thousands of bones littered the small town.

The Experts

Someone had to identify the corpses. But first they had to be put back together again. The town brought in a team of forensic anthropologists. They are experts at identifying human remains.

The Question
What would it take to get the remains back in their proper graves? And why did it matter?

Cover design: Maria Bergós, Book&Look **Interior design:** Red Herring Design/NYC

Photo Credits ©: cover top: Jeff Morgan 04/Alamy Images; 1: Charlie Riedel/AP Images; 2-3: Charlie Riedel/AP Images; 4-5: Tony Gutierrez/AP Images; 10 tombstone: MedicalRF.com/Getty Images; 13: Peter Newcomb/AFP/Getty Images; 14: Matt Slocum/AP Images; 17: David Lindroth, Inc.; 18 top: Jeff J. Mitchell/Getty Images; 18 bottom: Oli Scarff/Getty Images; 21, 22: Paul Sledzik/Disaster Mortuary Operational Response Team; 24: Tomas Bravo/Reuters; 26 background: Deco/Alamy Images; 26 bottom: Divine Images/Siri Stafford/Media Bakery; 29: Paul Sledzik; 31: Peter Brown; 32: Dominic Dibbs/Getty Images; 34: Tomas Bravo/Reuters; 36: Cliff Schiappa/AP Images; 37: Russell Kightley/Science Source; 38: Armed Forces Institute of Pathology; 40 top: Mauro Fermariello/Science Source; 40 center: Pascal Goetgheluck/Science Source; 40 right: JG Photography/Alamy Images; 41 top left: Paul Sancya/AP Images; 41 top right: David Hay Jones/Science Source; 41 bottom: Terrie Winson; 42-43: Roger Harris/Science Source; 44-45: Reuters.

All other photos © Shutterstock.

Library of Congress Cataloging-in-Publication Data
Names: Denega, Danielle, author.
Title: Floating skeletons : a small town is awash in bones / Danielle Denega.
Other titles: Dead men floating Description: [New edition] | New York : Children's Press/Scholastic, 2020.
| Series: Xbooks | Originally published: Dead men floating. New York, NY : Scholastic, 2011. | Audience:
Ages 8-10. | Audience: Grades 4-6. | Summary: "Book introduces the reader to Forensic Science"-- Provided
by publisher. Identifiers: LCCN 2020006036 | ISBN 9780531131701 (library binding)
| ISBN 9780531132593 (paperback) Subjects: LCSH: Forensic anthropology--Missouri--Hardin--Juvenile
literature. | Human remains (Archaeology)--Missouri--Hardin--Juvenile literature.
| Floods--Missouri--History--Juvenile literature. | Floods--Mississippi River Valley--History--Juvenile literature.
| Hardin (Mo.)--History--Juvenile literature.
Classification: LCC GN69.8 .D457 2020 | DDC 614/.17--dc23
LC record available at https://lccn.loc.gov/2020006036

No part of this publication may be reproduced in whole or in part, or stored in a retrieval system,
or transmitted in any form or by any means, electronic, mechanical, photocopying, recording, or otherwise,
without written permission of the publisher. For information regarding permission, write to Scholastic Inc.,
Attention: Permissions Department, Scholastic Inc., 557 Broadway, New York, NY 10012.

© 2021, 2012, 2007 Scholastic Inc.

All rights reserved. Published by Scholastic Inc.

Printed in Johor Bahru, Malaysia   108

1 2 3 4 5 6 7 8 9 10 R 30 29 28 27 26 25 24 23 22 21

SCHOLASTIC, XBOOKS, and associated logos are trademarks and/or registered trademarks of Scholastic Inc.

Scholastic Inc., 557 Broadway, New York, NY 10012.

FLOATING SKELETONS

A Small Town Is Awash in Bones

DANIELLE DENEGA

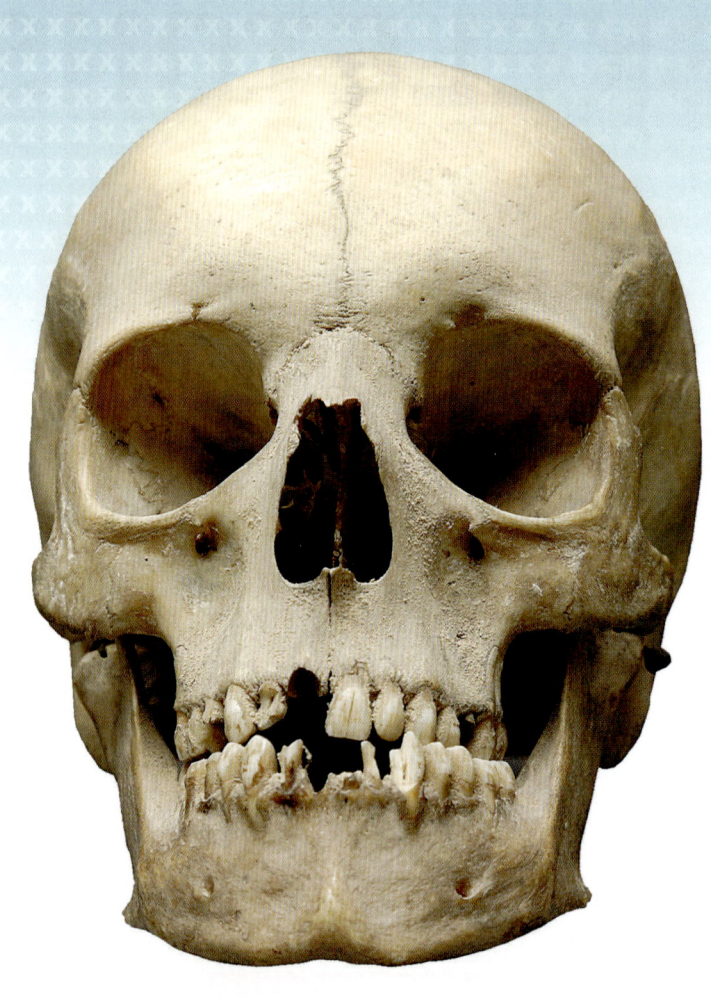

TABLE OF CONTENTS

PREVIEW **1**

CHAPTER 1
A Natural Disaster 10
At first the rain is a nuisance. Then it becomes a nightmare.

CHAPTER 2
Corpses on the Streets 14
A flood is coming—and there is nothing anyone can do to stop it.

Map **17**

CHAPTER 3
Bringing the Dead to Life 18
Experts try to get a picture of the bodies from the cemetery.

Bone Detective **24**

CHAPTER 4
Close-Up on Corpses 26
Forensic experts begin to sort and study the remains.

Skull & Bones **30**

CHAPTER 5
Putting the Pieces Together 32
Hardin's dead can rest in peace again.

XFILES **37**
ID Expert **38**
Body Scan **40**
Bare Bones **42**

1

A Natural Disaster

At first the rain is a nuisance. Then it becomes a nightmare.

When rain started falling in the midwestern United States during the spring of 1993, no one could have imagined the devastation it would bring. Storm after storm pummeled the region. Rivers began to overflow their banks. Throughout the summer, floodwaters destroyed homes and businesses. Roads and bridges were washed away.

The flooding didn't end until the fall. By then, more than 500 counties in nine midwestern states had been hit hard. Floodwaters covered more than 20 million acres (8 million hectares) of land.

Home Wrecker

The wreckage from the flood was terrible. Fifty people died, and 55,000 homes were damaged or destroyed. The flood caused more than $15 billion in damage. Much of the Midwest was declared a disaster area.

The event became known as the Great Flood of 1993. It was one of the worst natural disasters in American history. And the horrors it unleashed would forever haunt one small Missouri town.

PART OF HIGHWAY 40 in Missouri was underwater when the Missouri River flooded in 1993.

VIEW OF A CEMETERY flooded by a storm.

2

Corpses on the Streets

**A flood is coming—
and there is nothing anyone
can do to stop it.**

Hardin is only six miles (10 kilometers) north of the Missouri River. So people there knew that it was only a matter of time before the flood reached their town.

That horrible day came in July 1993. The rushing waters swept through Hardin, destroying homes and other buildings. Then something so terrible happened that the town would never be the same.

Digging Up the Dead

At the time, there was a small cemetery in Hardin. It had been built in a low-lying area in 1828. It was where most of the town's approximately 600 residents buried their dead.

When the flood hit, water rushed into Hardin Cemetery. It poured into the graves and dug up the coffins. Hundreds of headstones, burial vaults, and coffins were swept away. About half of the 1,576 graves in the cemetery were destroyed.

Even worse, hundreds of coffins broke open. Human remains spilled out and floated through the streets and fields. Some ended up as far as 18 miles (29 km) away.

The people of Hardin were powerless to stop the raging flood and the destruction of the cemetery. They watched in horror as water washed away the bodies of their loved ones. "People are just heartsick," one resident said to a reporter.

HARDIN, MISSOURI, is located six miles north of the Missouri River.

IN DEPTH

Hardin, Missouri

The Missouri River overflowed its banks in the Great Flood of 1993. The flood left much of the Midwest underwater.

IN A FLOODED AREA, divers can sometimes help gather human remains.

3

Bringing the Dead to Life

Experts try to get a picture of the bodies from the cemetery.

It was like a scene from a horror movie. Some of the corpses in Hardin were newer and whole. Others had been buried more than a century before. Those remains had broken apart and scattered across town.

The people of Hardin needed help. So they turned to Dean Snow, the county coroner. They wanted him to identify the remains so their loved ones could be laid to rest once more.

Snow organized a special team. It was made up of members of DMORT, or the Disaster Mortuary Operational Response Team. They are a team of experts put together by the U.S. government to help identify bodies after major accidents.

Snow's team included forensic anthropologists. Those are scientists who help identify human remains. The team also included forensic pathologists. Those are medical experts who figure out how a person died.

The team members' mission was clear. They had to find and identify the remains from the cemetery.

Searching for Remains

The first step was to search for these remains. With the help of volunteers from Hardin, team members found nearly 600 coffins. They recovered 3,400 bones, including 129 skulls. They stored the remains in barns and refrigerated trucks at the county fairgrounds.

Next, the team created antemortem profiles of the missing dead. *Antemortem* means "before death." The profiles included information gathered about the people before they died, such as dental and medical

A MEMBER OF the Disaster Mortuary Operational Response Team views the destruction at Hardin Cemetery during the 1993 flood.

records. These records could help the team match identities to remains. For example, if an antemortem profile showed that a person had once broken his leg, the experts would look for a skeleton with that injury.

There was just one problem. For many of the missing dead, dental and medical records were not available.

Paul Sledzik was a forensic anthropologist from the DMORT team. "In the Hardin disaster," Sledzik explained, "many of the missing had been dead for a very long time."

Dearly Departed

Investigators tried to fill in the gaps. They asked people to describe their missing relatives. Did the dead have any broken bones? What clothes had they been buried in?

Their answers helped the investigators create antemortem profiles for most of the people who had been buried in the cemetery.

Matching the corpses and bones to the profiles was the next step.

ANTHROPOLOGISTS EXAMINE pelvic bones collected from Hardin Cemetery after the flood.

Bone Detective

Here's a step-by-step guide to how a forensic anthropologist matches bones to a missing person.

IN DEPTH

1. **Clean the bones.**
   Use flesh-eating beetles to remove any flesh on the bones. If there is a rush, boil the bones in soapy water instead.

2. **Confirm that the bones are human.**
   Anthropologists can tell the difference between the bones of a human and another animal.

3. **Identify the bones.**
   Decide what part of the body each bone came from. Then "side" the bones—figure out whether each bone came from the left or right side of the body. Finally, lay the bones out the way they would appear if the skeleton were intact.

4. **Examine the bones.**
   Measure, weigh, and x-ray the bones. Study them under a microscope.

5. **Create a postmortem profile.**
   Postmortem means "after death." By examining just a few bones, experts can determine a dead person's age, height, race, and gender. Bones can also reveal how long the person has been dead and what may have caused the death.

6. **Compare the profile to the antemortem records.**
   Look at the missing person's medical records. Do the details match the postmortem profile?

4

Close-Up on Corpses

Forensic experts begin to sort and study the remains.

The DMORT team had finished the antemortem profiles. Now it was time to create postmortem profiles. These postmortem profiles were records of what the team had learned about the corpses and bones.

Team members would then compare the postmortem profiles to the antemortem profiles and try to find matches. That way, they could identify the corpses.

The remains were in various states of decay. Some were new and well preserved. Some were dried up like mummies. Some were skeletons. Others were just pieces of bones. A forensic pathologist handled the bodies that had a lot of soft tissue left. The anthropology team handled the remains that were mostly bones.

Inside the Coffins

Thirty-five of the coffins held complete skeletons. The anthropologists measured the skulls and the long bones. (Those are bones that are longer than they are wide and are rounded at both ends.)

Personal items, such as watches or blankets, were often found inside the coffins. That information was added to the postmortem profiles.

Some bodies had been torn from their coffins. Sledzik and the others did what they could to create profiles of these skeletons. They measured bones to figure out a person's age, race, gender, and height. The anthropologists also looked for evidence of broken bones or diseases. But these were the easy cases. Others would turn out to be more difficult—and gruesome.

SKULLS ARE LINED UP at the morgue that was set up outside Hardin.

Skull & Bones

The skeleton is the bony framework of the body. When people are born, they have more than 300 bones. As they grow, some of those bones join together. Adults have only about 206 bones.

Human Skeleton

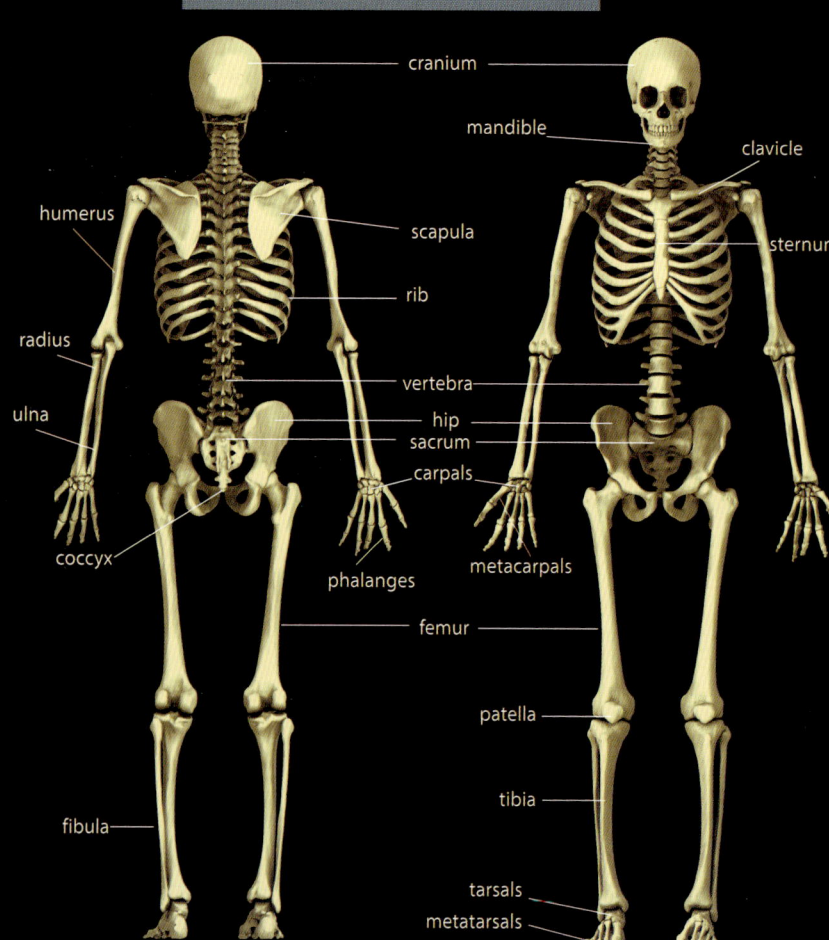

IN DEPTH

The cranium, or upper part of the skull, holds and protects the brain. Eight bony plates form the human cranium. They fit together at joints called sutures. The human head also includes 14 facial bones that form the lower front of the skull. They provide the framework for most of the face.

Human Skull

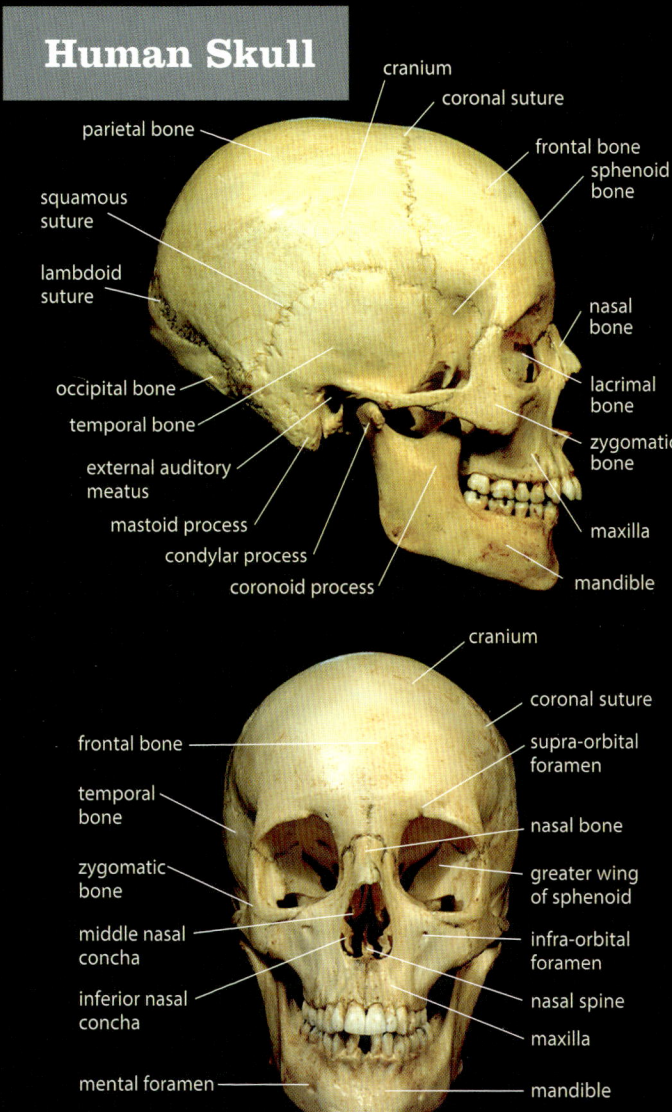

A COFFIN is being buried underground

5

Putting the Pieces Together

Hardin's dead can rest in peace again.

Paul Sledzik and his team continued their work on the postmortem profiles. They turned to the hundreds of loose bones they had found. All of the bits and pieces had to be sorted.

The forensic anthropologists sorted the bones by type. They put skulls in one place. Tibias—bones found in the shins—were put in another area. Femurs—thighbones—were grouped together, and so on.

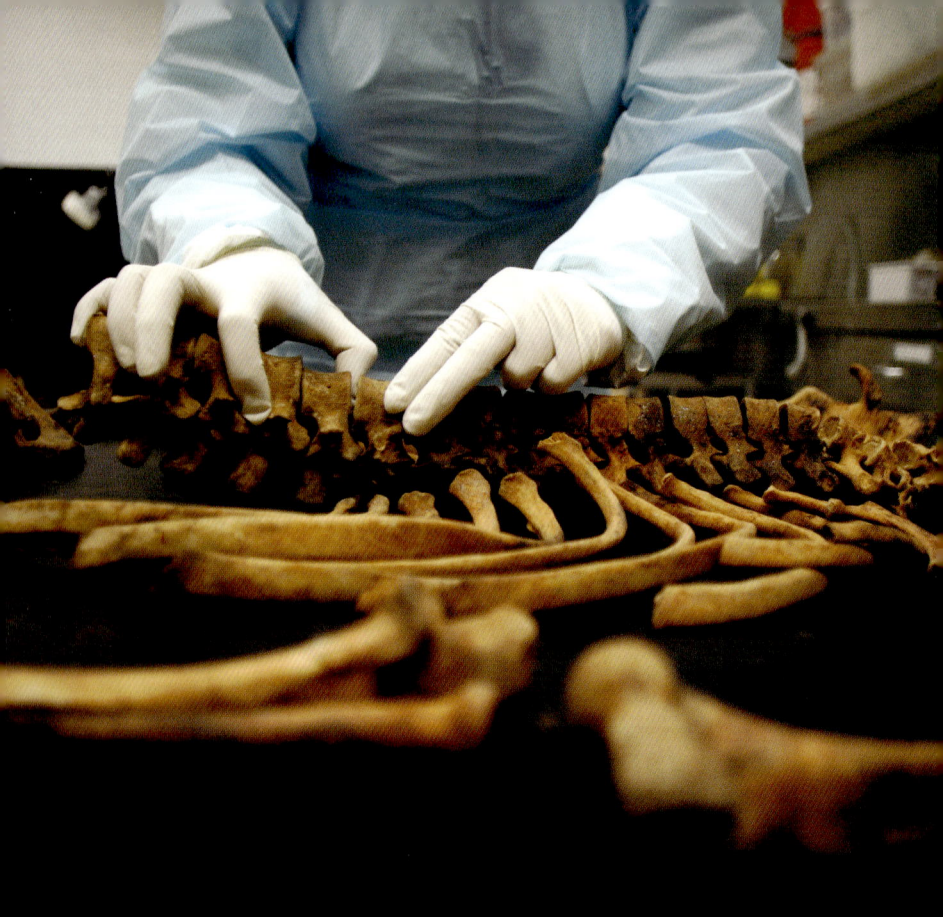

A FORENSIC ANTHROPOLOGIST
pieces together a human skeleton

After sorting the bones, the anthropologists tried to "side" them. That's the process of figuring out whether a bone is from the left or right side of the body.

Next, the experts grouped the bones according to age. Finally, they tried to separate males from females.

The team found it nearly impossible to put together whole skeletons. However, they were able to estimate the number of people whose remains they found. The flood had washed away the remains of 793 people. The team estimated that they had found about 600 of these bodies.

Personal Profiles

As the team members finished examining the remains, they moved on to their final task. They compared the postmortem profiles to the antemortem profiles. Slowly, they began to identify bodies.

Some cases were easy to solve. A well-preserved body might be identified by a tattoo. A coffin could be linked to a name by a piece of jewelry found inside.

In the end, Sledzik and the rest of the DMORT team identified the remains of 120 people.

By October 1993, the DMORT team had left town. The people of Hardin prepared to rebury remains. For those that could not be identified, bones and pieces of bones were placed in 476 separate vaults. Each vault was carefully tagged so it could be linked with its postmortem profile.

Vernie Fountain led a team of funeral directors who helped respond to the disaster. He told the *New York Times* that the flood had been terrible for the families of the missing dead. "You bury someone and you expect them to be buried for eternity," he said.

Today, there are two memorials at the Hardin Cemetery. One is a tribute to the courage and dedication of the people of Hardin. The other is for all the people who were displaced by the flood. **X**

A MEMORIAL STANDS IN THE CEMETERY close to a pond that was created by the floodwaters.

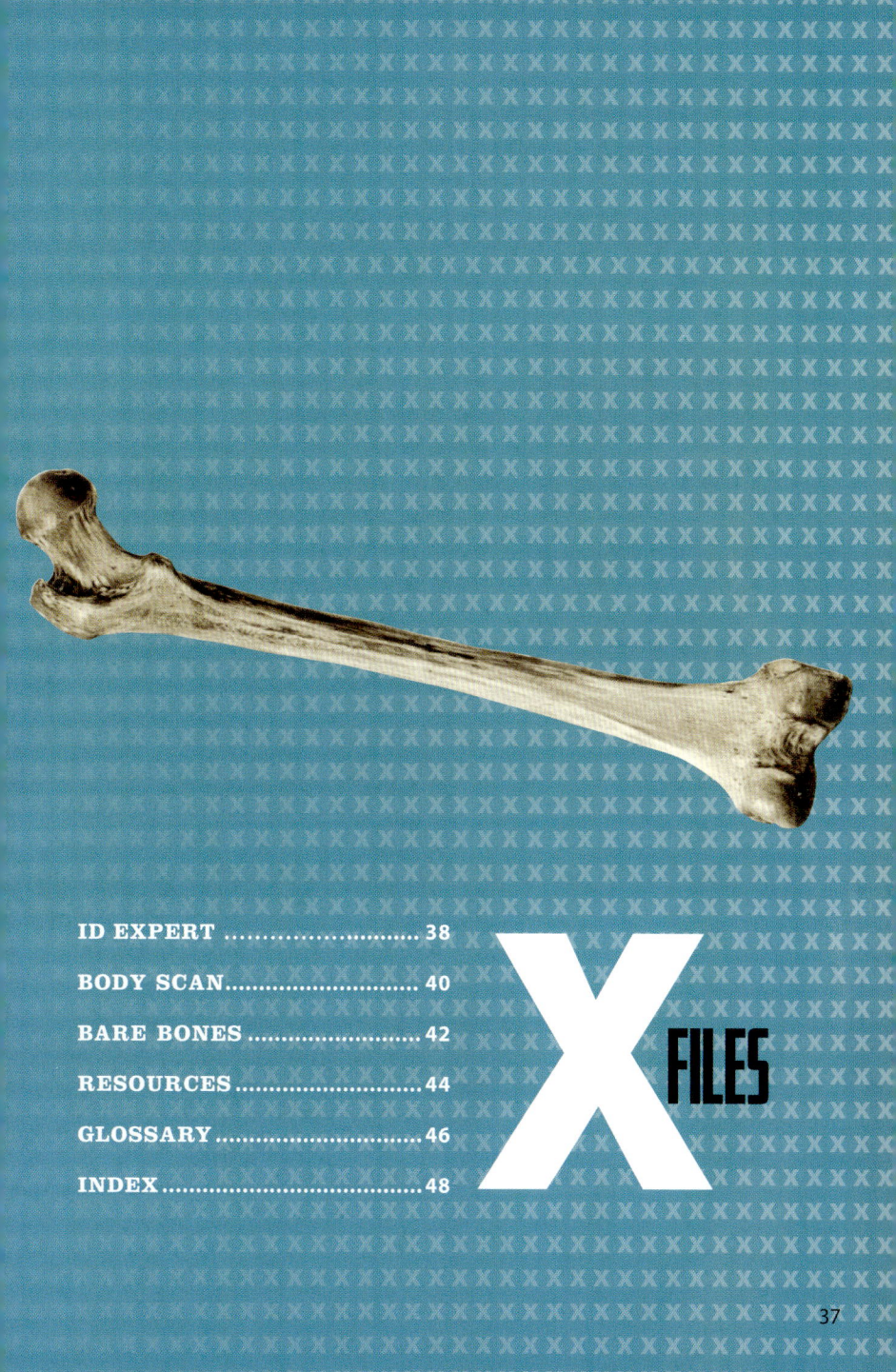

ID EXPERT	38
BODY SCAN	40
BARE BONES	42
RESOURCES	44
GLOSSARY	46
INDEX	48

X FILES

ID Expert

Forensic anthropologist Paul Sledzik identifies the dead for a living.

PAUL SLEDZIK works for the National Transportation Safety Board in Washington, D.C.

How did you become interested in anthropology?

SLEDZIK: I had always had an interest in biology, history, archeology, and human evolution. Then I had a really interesting anthropology professor. I was hooked.

How did you get into the forensic side of anthropology?

SLEDZIK: I did a few forensic cases with the college professor I liked. But most of my forensic experience came from the Armed Forces Institute of Pathology. That's where I learned the techniques and applications of the field.

What does a forensic anthropologist do?

SLEDZIK: Most forensic anthropologists work on individual skeletal cases. I tend to look at disaster situations. I make sure different agencies work together to identify victims of disasters. I work with family members, federal government officials, and scientists.

IN DEPTH

How is forensic anthropology useful in large disasters?

SLEDZIK: First, forensic anthropologists identify remains. Second, they help with the search and recovery. Third, they help manage the overall identification efforts.

What questions do you ask at a mass disaster site?

SLEDZIK: Are you dealing with whole bodies or parts of bodies? Are the bodies spread over a large area or in a small site? Is it a closed population disaster? (Plane crashes are a closed population disaster because you know how many people were on the plane.) Or is it an open population disaster—and you don't know how many people were involved?

Is it hard to work with family members of the victims?

SLEDZIK: It can be. Loved ones have to provide us with a lot of information. We, in turn, need to keep them informed about what's going on.

Are there other challenges?

SLEDZIK: Sure. We have to get antemortem information to make an identification. In cases like Hurricane Katrina, records were flooded. So the information wasn't available.

What advice would you give students who are interested in forensic anthropology?

SLEDZIK: Figure out what you really like about forensic science. Many TV shows portray it in a glamorous way. In reality it's a lot of lab work. You aren't working with criminals. You're working with information and data and samples. So, if it's the glamour that you're after, it may not be for you!

What is the most interesting part of your job?

SLEDZIK: I like not knowing what will happen day to day. There could be an accident in the next hour that I have to go out to. Or I could get a call from a family member with a unique question. Or there could be a call from a medical examiner with information about a new aspect of victim identification.

Body Scan

Check out a forensic anthropologist's tools of the trade.

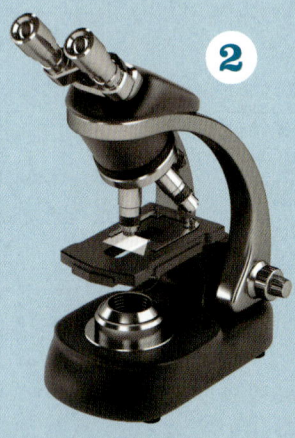

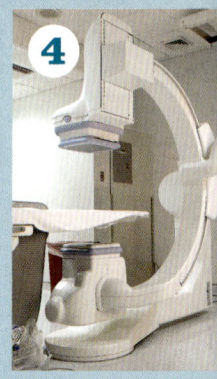

1 Caliper: This tool is used to measure the size of bones.

2 Microscope: Anthropologists sometimes have to look for details that can't be seen with the naked eye.

3 FORDISC (forensic discriminant) software: Anthropologists use this program to help determine the race and gender of a skull. They type in different measurements from a skull. The computer does the rest.

4 X-ray machine: This device uses high-energy beams to create images of teeth, bones, and organs inside the body.

IN DEPTH

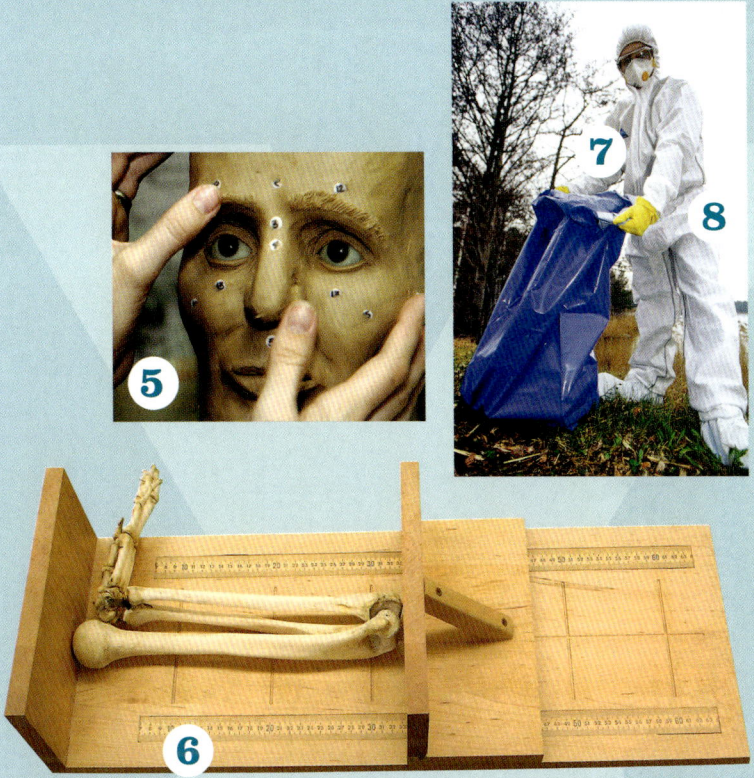

5 Clay, wig, prosthetic eyes: Forensic anthropologists use these when they do facial reconstruction on a human skull.

6 Osteometric board: This tool is used to find the lengths of the long bones of a skeleton.

7 Latex gloves: Anthropologists wear protective gloves when they handle evidence.

8 Tyvek suit: Anthropologists wear this suit when they work with remains. It protects against dangerous germs. Tyvek is nearly impossible to tear. It allows only water vapor to pass through.

Bare Bones

Here's how forensic anthropologists get information from bones.

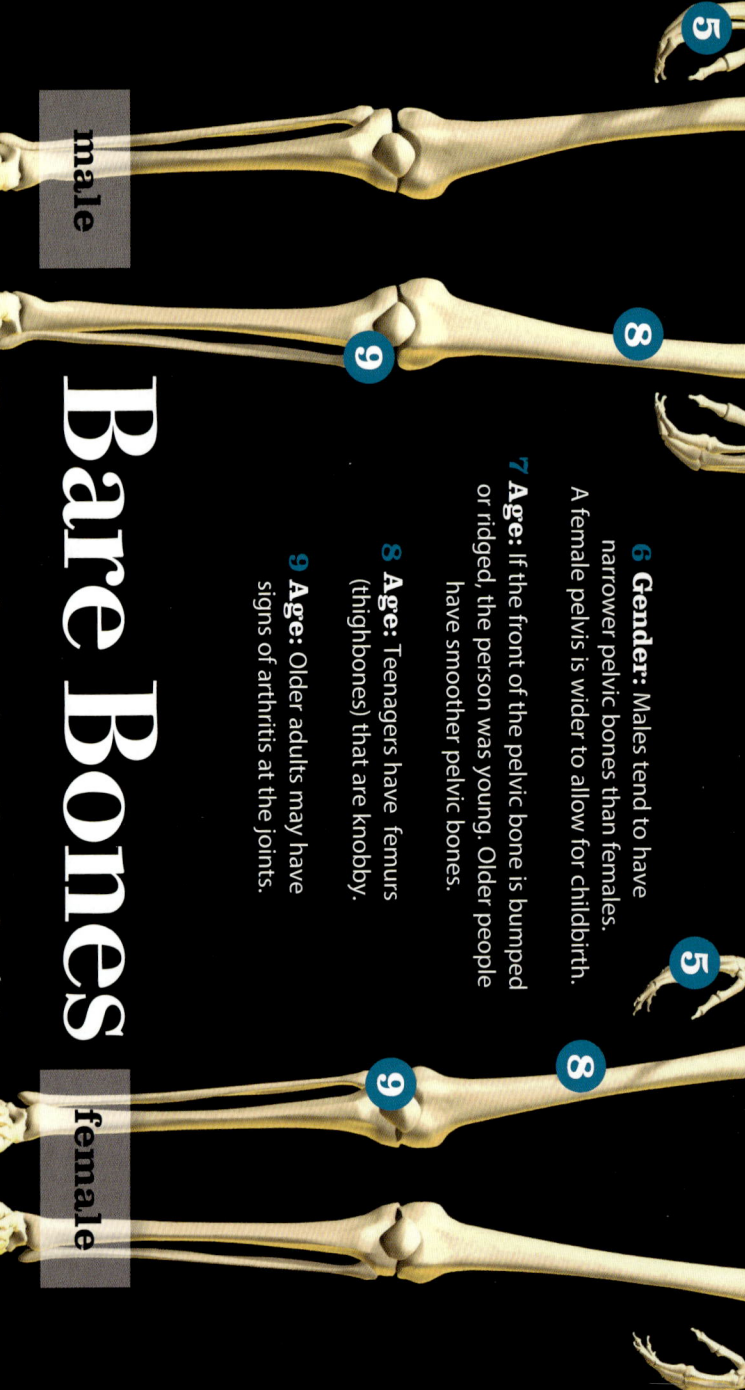

6 Gender: Males tend to have narrower pelvic bones than females. A female pelvis is wider to allow for childbirth.

7 Age: If the front of the pelvic bone is bumped or ridged, the person was young. Older people have smoother pelvic bones.

8 Age: Teenagers have femurs (thighbones) that are knobby.

9 Age: Older adults may have signs of arthritis at the joints.

IN DEPTH

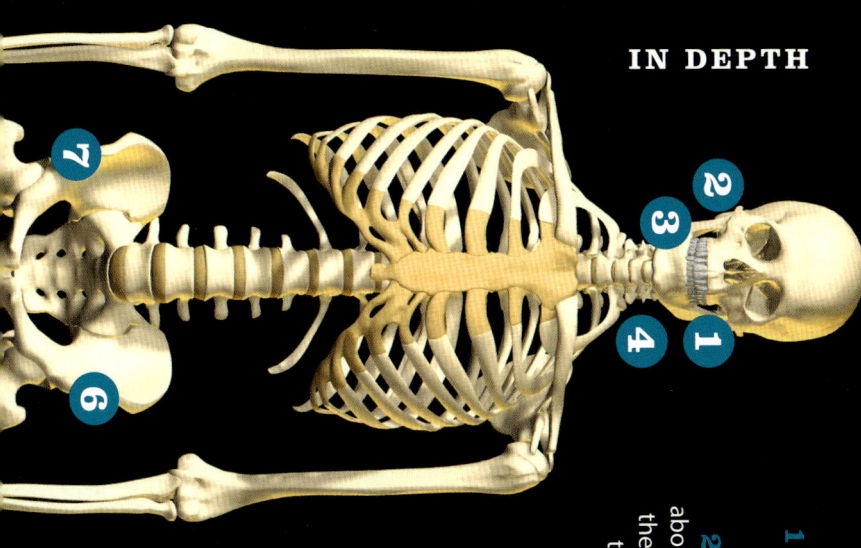

1. **Gender:** Male jaws tend to be square. Female jaws are more pointed.

2. **Race:** Anthropologists can get clues about a person's race from the length of the jaw, the distance between the eyes, the openings in the nose, and the slant of the cheekbones.

3. **Is it human?** Are the back teeth dull and the front teeth sharper? If so, they belonged to a human.

4. **Age:** Small children have baby teeth. Older children have permanent teeth. In older adults the teeth may be worn down.

5. **Occupation:** When muscles get heavy use, bony ridges form where the muscle attaches to the bone. People who worked with their hands might have noticeable ridges on the bones of their wrists.

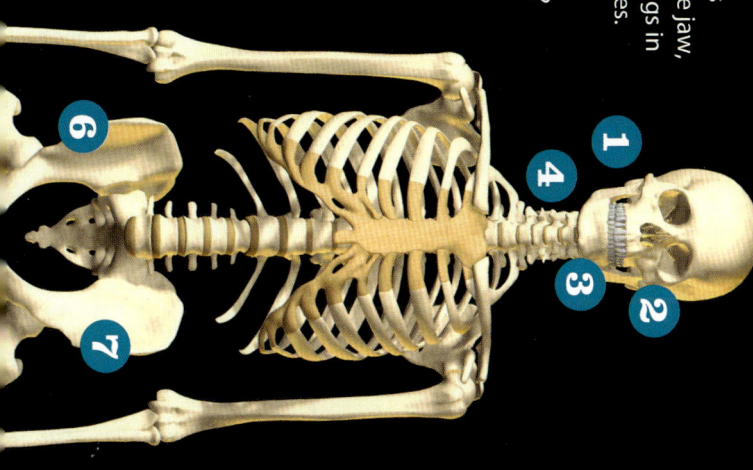

RESOURCES

Here's a selection of books for more information about bones and forensic science.

NONFICTION

Bedell, J. M. *So, You Want to Work with the Ancient and Recent Dead?: Unearthing Careers from Paleontology to Forensic Science (Be What You Want)*. New York: Aladdin, 2015.

Colson, Rob Scott. *Bone Collection: Skulls*. New York: Scholastic, 2014.

Denega, Danielle. *Skulls and Skeletons (24/7: Science Behind the Scenes: Forensics)*. New York: Scholastic, 2007.

Jenkins, Steve. *Bones: Skeletons and How They Work*. New York: Scholastic, 2010.

Latta, Sara. *Bones: Dead People Do Tell Tales (True Forensic Crime Stories)*. New York: Enslow, 2012.

MacLeod, Elizabeth. *Bones Never Lie: How Forensics Helps Solve History's Mysteries*. Toronto: Annick Press, 2013.

Ollhoff, Jim. *DNA: Window to the Past (Your Family Tree)*. Minneapolis: Abdo, 2011.

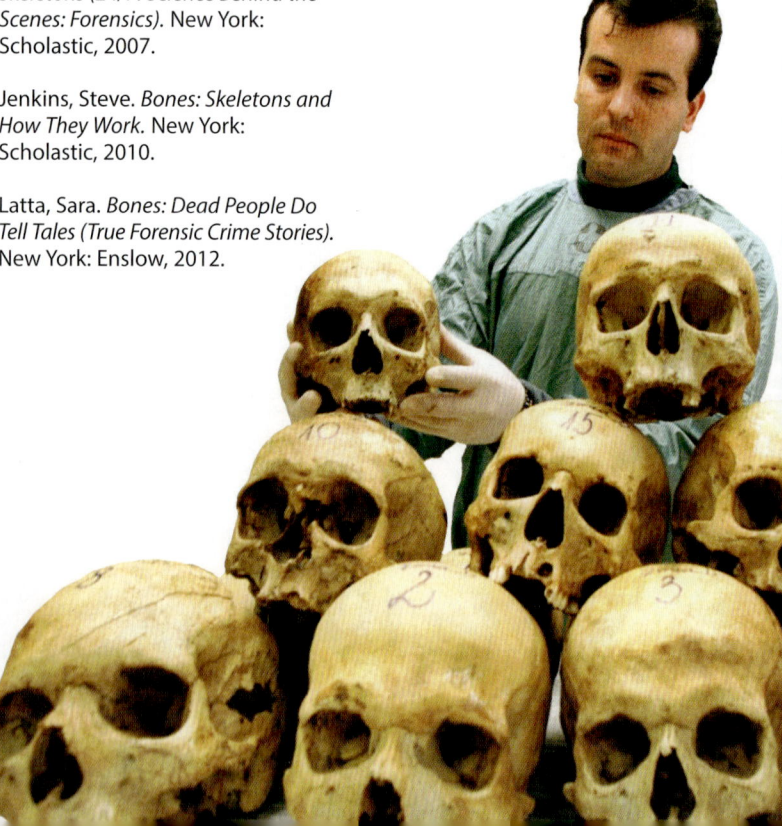

FICTION

Grisham, John. *Theodore Boone: Kid Lawyer*. New York: Dutton, 2010.

Harris, Robert. *Artie Conan Doyle and the Gravediggers' Club (The Artie Conan Doyle Mysteries)*. Edinburgh: Kelpies, 2017.

Heide, Florence Parry. *Mystery at Blue Ridge Cemetery (Spotlight Club Mysteries)*. Park Ridge, Illinois: Albert Whitman, 2013.

Keene, Carolyn. *The Stolen Bones (Nancy Drew: All New Girl Detective)*. New York: Aladdin, 2008.

Manhein, Mary H. *Claire Carter, Bone Detective: The Mystery of the Bones in the Drainpipe*. Louisiana: Os Liber Press, 2018.

Richards, Jame. *Three Rivers Rising: A Novel of the Johnstown Flood*. New York: Knopf, 2010.

Uhlberg, Myron. *A Storm Called Katrina*. Atlanta: Peachtree Publishing Company, 2015.

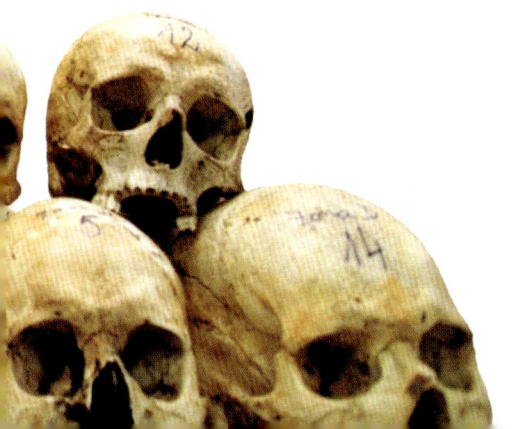

GLOSSARY

antemortem (an-tee-MORE-tuhm) *adjective* before death

anthropology (an-thruh-POL-uh-jee) *noun* the study of human beings, including their bones, language, and culture

arthritis (ar-THRY-tis) *noun* a disease that causes sore, inflamed, or stiffened joints

cemetery (SEM-uh-teh-ree) *noun* a place where people are buried after they die

corpse (KORPS) *noun* a dead human body

cranium (KRAY-nee-uhm) *noun* another word for *skull*, especially the part that covers the brain

decay (di-KAY) *noun* the breaking down of plant or animal matter by natural causes

devastation (dev–uh-STAY-shun) *noun* severe damage or destruction

DMORT (DEE-mort) *noun* a team of experts who help identify victims and prepare them for burial after big disasters or accidents; DMORT stands for *Disaster Mortuary Operational Response Team*

evidence (EV-uh-denss) *noun* materials gathered during an investigation that provide clues

expert (EKS-purt) *noun* a person who has knowledge and experience in a certain field

femur (FEE-mur) *noun* the thighbone

forensic anthropologist (fuh-REN-sik an-thruh-POL-uh-jist) *noun* a scientist who studies bones and uses that knowledge in investigations

forensic anthropology (fuh-REN-sik an-thruh-POL-uh-jee) *noun* the study and use of bone knowledge in investigations

forensic pathologist (fuh-REN-sik path-OL-uh-jist) *noun* a medical expert who determines the official cause and manner of death

gender (JEN-dur) *noun* the behavioral, cultural, or psychological traits typically associated with one sex

identify (eye-DEN-tuh-fye) *verb* to establish who someone is or what something is

joint (JOINT) *noun* a place where two bones meet

long bone (LONG BONE) *noun* a bone that has a long shaft and knobs on both ends

microscope (MYE-kruh-skope) *noun* a tool that makes objects appear larger so they can be studied

pelvic bone (PEL-vik BONE) *noun* a hip bone

postmortem (pohst-MORE-tuhm) *adjective* after death

pummel (PUHM-uhl) *verb* to strike something or someone repeatedly

remains (ri-MAYNZ) *noun* dead bodies

skeleton (SKEL-uh-tuhn) *noun* the bony framework of the body

skull (SKUHL) *noun* the bony frame of the head

sutures (SOO-churz) *noun* joints that hold the bones of the skull together

tibia (TIH-bee-uh) *noun* one of the two bones in the shin

tissue (TISH-oo) *noun* a fabric of the same kind of cells. There are four main kinds: muscles, tissue made up of muscle cells; epithelial tissue, which covers the surface of the body; connective tissue, which helps support and join together parts of the body; and nervous tissue, which carries nerve signals throughout the body.

unearth (uhn-URTH) *verb* to dig up

vault (VAWLT) *noun* an underground burial chamber

x-ray (EKS-ray) *verb* to photograph a body part with radiation, which allows doctors and scientists to see through skin

INDEX

age, 25, 28, 35, 42
animal bones, 25, 43
antemortem profiles, 20, 23, 25, 27, 35, 39
Armed Forces Institute of Pathology, 38

bones, 20, *22*, 23, *24*, 25, *26*, 27–28, *29*, *30–31*, 33, *34*, 35, 36, 40, 41, *41*, *42–43*

calipers, 40, *40*
cemetery. *See* Hardin Cemetery.
clay, 41, *41*
closed population disasters, 39
coffins, 16, 20, 28, *32*, 35
computers, 40, *40*
coroner, 19
corpses, 16, 19, 23, 27–28

damage, 11, 12, 15, 16
decay, 28
dental records, 20, 23
Disaster Mortuary Operational Response Team (DMORT), 20, *21*, *22*, 23, 27, 28, 33, 35, 36

facial bones, 31, *31*
facial reconstructions, 41, *41*
family members, 16, 19, 23, 38, 39
flesh-eating beetles, 25
flood. *See* Great Flood of 1993.
FORDISC software, 40, *40*
forensic anthropologists, 20, *22*, 23, *24*, 25, 28, 33, *34*, 35, 38–39, *38*, 40–41, *42–43*
forensic pathologists, 20, 28
Fountain, Vernie, 36
funeral directors, 36

gender, 25, 28, 35, 40, 42, 43
germs, 41
graves, 16
Great Flood of 1993, 11–12, *13*, *14*, 15, 16, *17*, *18*, *21*, 36

Hardin Cemetery, *14*, 16, 20, *21*, *22*, 23

Hardin, Missouri, *14*, 15–16, *17*, 19, 20, *21*, *22*, 23, *29*, 33, 36
Hurricane Katrina, 39

identification, 19, 20, 23, 25, 27–28, 35, 36, 38, 39

latex gloves, 41, *41*

map, *17*
medical records, 20, 23, 25, 39
microscopes, 25, 40, *40*
Missouri River, *13*, 15, *17*

news reports, 16, 36

occupations, 43
open population disasters, 39
osteometric boards, 41, *41*

personal items, 23, 28, 35
postmortem profiles, 25, 27, 28, 33, 35, 36
prosthetic eyes, 41, *41*

race, 25, 28, 40, 43
remains, 16, 19, 20, 23, 27, 28, 35–36, 39, 41
reconstructions, 25, 41, *41*

"siding," 25, 35
skulls, 20, *24*, *26*, 28, *29*, *31*, 33, 40, 41
Sledzik, Paul, 23, 28, 33, 35, 38–39, *38*
Snow, Dean, 19–20
sorting, 33, *34*, 35
storms, 11, 39
sutures, 31

tools, 40–41, *40*, *41*
Tyvek suits, 41, *41*

vaults, 16, 36, *36*
volunteers, 20

wigs, 41

x-rays, 25, 40, *40*

48